EVE SONG

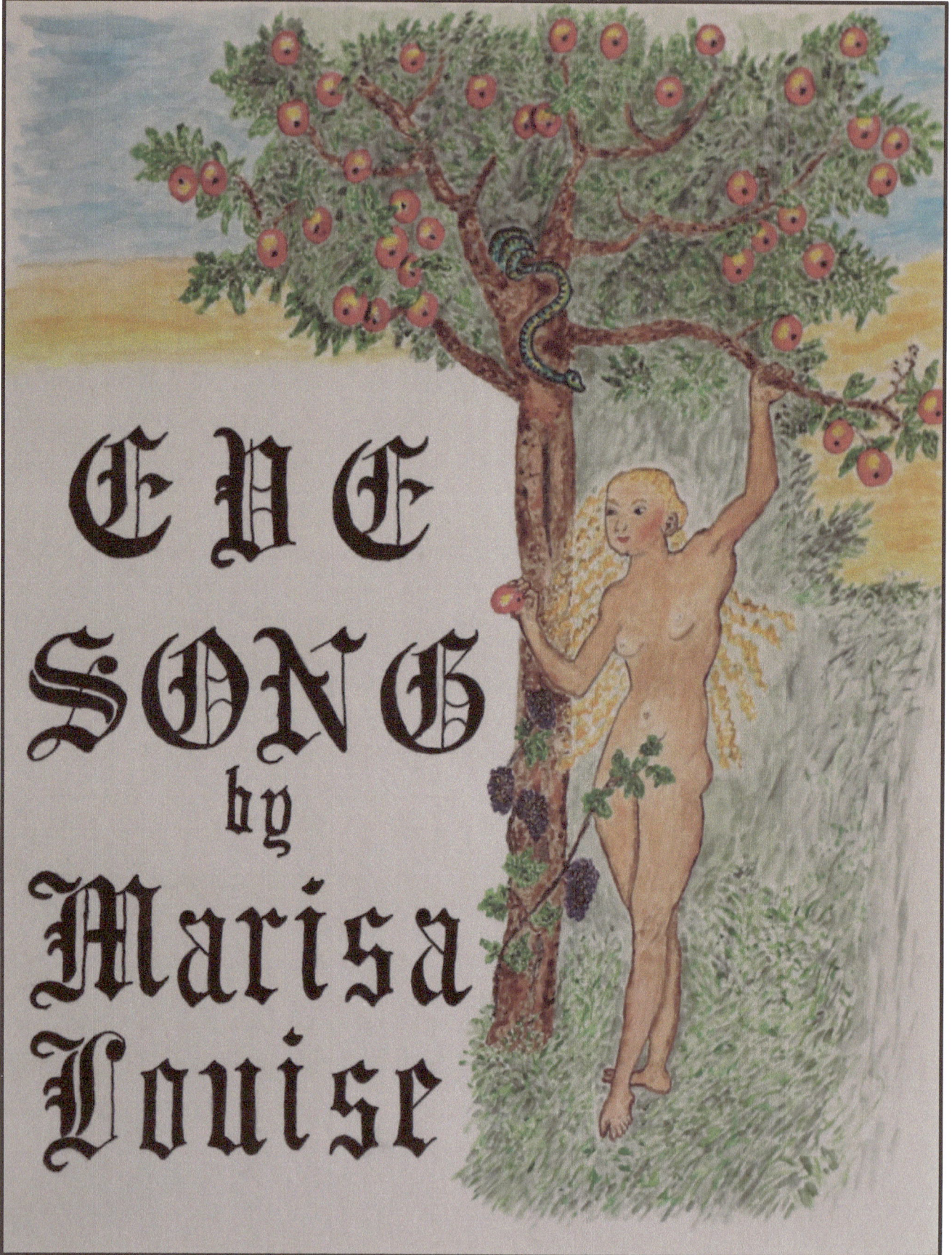

EVE SONG

by Marisa Louise

Harnessing Creativity Press

Copyright © 2021 Mary-Louise Hansen
Cover art and illustrations by Marisa Louise

All Rights reserved. No part of this publication may be reproduced, stored in a retrieval system, or transmitted, in any form or by any means, electronic, mechanical, photocopying, recording, or otherwise, without the prior permission of the publisher.
Harnessing Creativity Press
561 Santa Barbara Rd.
Berkeley, CA 94707

ISBN 978-1-7376030-2-3

Printed in the United States of America

In memory of Yakov Malkiel

Can vei la lauzeta mover
de joi sas alas contral rai,
que s'oblid' e's laissa chazer
per la doussor c'al cor li vai,
ai! tan grans enveya m'en ve
de cui qu'eu veya jauzion,
meravilhas ai, car desse
lo cor de dezirer no'm fon.

When I see the lark beat
for joy his wings against the sun ray
so that he forgets and allows himself to fall
from the sweetness that comes to his heart
Ah! what great envy comes to me
of whoever I see who is joyful,
I marvel that from this
my heart doesn't melt me from desire.

Bernart de Ventadorn (1150-80)

CONTENTS

Frozen Rainbows	9
Sun Rose	11
Crescent	13
Paisley	15
When I See the Lark	17
Flower Children	21
Nectar of the Gods	25
This is the Way that Love Dies	27
Forgotten Angel	31
Bridge of Illusion	35
There are no Roses without Thorns	37
Prayer to the Virgin	41
Life in Rose	47
Silent Prisons	53
Estranged	59
Walkabout in the Dreamtime	63
Mother Hood Reflection	67
Capturing Bubbles	71

Catherine Wheel	75
Patchwork	83
Magic Mirror	89
Cassandra	95
Dance with Death	105
Lucy Indigo	111
The Smile	117
Fifth Commandment	121
Electra	127
Night Train	137
Phantom Riches	143
Ode to Sappho	149
Moon Daughter	153
Time Elapse	157
Sea Salt	163
Atonal Atonement	167
Steel Dinosaur Apocalypse	171
Hippocampus Homecoming	175

Frozen Rainbows

Icy rivers creep down,
And with them my rainbows
To freeze into waterfalls
Of dripping icicles;
In ethereal blue
Of a night-washed sea
Blown, bubble-eyed fish
Bathe in frozen patterns,
Painted, faded by frigid frost.

Laughing children into silence,
Like fluttering petals of irises
Floating down between dulled spears;
Sunlit colors
To violet fluorescence,
Voices echoing
Into jagged-edge hoarfrost,
Shatter with a tinkle of glass chimes,
Forgotten under the ice,
Frozen impenetrably.

Sun Rose

Folding in upon itself
Lances of light
To golden heart of dawn;
Unfurling sunset petals
In dying ripples
Of a wild birth song;
Gold to red, drooping head,
Dropping colored leaves, dead,
Exposing a withered, barren heart,
Pierced in the darkness
By spears of stars,
Who sang in cold silver voices
Long silent.

Crescent

In the charm of a smile, Coquette,
As the horned moon rocks to a violin's waltz,
And wavelets lap a gondola's black arc,
Capricious sunlight is captured for a moment;
Multiplied in transient rainbows: paper lanterns
Sway gently in warm night air.

As delicate white fingers divide a golden orange,
Sweet ambrosia fragrance blends
With soft strumming of lutes;
The whisper of a dream, as eyes close in sleep,
Floating on silent wings high above in ethereal sky.

Waltzing together, in embrace encircled,
Two masks meet in a kiss.
Suspended in ripples of laughter,
A juggler's bright balloons
Join together in myriad shapes of clubs,
Reversing to diamonds in the strobe of perception.

In fluttering breezes of your fan,
Affections, like colorful pinwheels, spin,
Unfurling to roses of intoxicating perfume,
In a shower of golden pollen, to the morning sun,
Which shatters rainbow crystals,
Distilling a drop of sweet nectar.

Paisley

Bitter salt tears,

Raining from a bruised heart,

Venomous drops of blood that permeate the mind:

Drink the draught of intoxicating wine

From a bleeding heart,

Crushed by lust, like grapes of Arcadia.

Spirits of temptation, conjured up in the flames

Of a burning soul

Whirl through fumes,

And in their midst, the dark, sensuous

Queen of Death.

Like mushroom hallucinations, all disappears,

As smoke spirals slowly up

Through stagnant air.

The heart pulses with healing force,

Gentle growth of green buds,

Bulbs inverted deep in rich, purple earth:

With the breath of life, yin and yang,

Fish leap in cool, blue waves,

And butterflies fill the dizzy, spring air.

When I See the Lark

pour le docteur Bonquilui

Praise to the magician who,
With the whisper of a spell,
Instills in all nature the spirit of animation,
The breath of fresh wind that dissipates fog,
Revealing dizzy blue of a sunlit sky;
The puff of air that billows sails
And fills balloons to drift up through a crystal stratosphere;
The breeze laden with far-away sounds and scents
That awakens children of joy,
Setting bells to ringing
In a lace-work chaos of carillon patterns.

The mist of first rain that seeps into the earth,
Restoring shriveled roots,
Giving new life to drooping leaves,
Like a hero's drink of strength from holy vessels;
The diviner's rod that taps the springs,
Filling pools of the soul with refreshing coolness;

The energy to an electric light
That makes it glow with brilliance,
The match that kindles fire,
The sunbeam that opens a flower bud,
Letting out a breath of perfume.

The flames that heat the forge of creation,
Re-activating hammer and tongs:
The heat that thaws snow,
Melting icy blue spirits
Of fear, self-contempt, and depression,
Who held fast the wheels of imagination,
Opening doors frozen shut
To free the spirit,

Bubbling out in volcanic eruption of joyful emotions,

While Ambition, harnessed to the carriage of Will,

Leaps forward,

And Inspiration flies out

On wings of ecstasy.

Flower Children

Dandy lion girl with shimmering gold hair,
Blooming on the path of a haunting nightmare,
I wait for a message in the parlor bare-
headed for the door, but hovering in the snare.
I nibble a fig, you are silent in your chair,
But your eyes are telling me I shouldn't be there.
I'll sip dandelion wine as long as I dare,
For the song of the siren is sweet and fair.

Flower children in a psychedelic dream,
Spinning in auras like a sun-and-moonbeam.
Mirage in the desert of a barren mind:
I stand on a threshold, filled with joy I find,
But no one leads me in, so I can't pass the door,
For it's only a mirror of my own inner core.

Poppies in the grass and morning glories blue
Open their hearts to the sunny view,
Rosy visions of those innocent few
Who bask in pleasures, re-discovered anew,
Of childhood joys that never grew.
Rooted in earth, but floating too
In a lotus dream from an herbal brew,
Nirvana of oblivion to grief and rue.

Jellyfish maidens glow with iridescent light,
In champagne mist on a glass sea of night,
Through the wake of a cruising barge they glide,
And wash ashore in words of the tide;
They stand for a moment, trembling and white,
'Til they dry to paper shells in the sun so bright,
All that remains of a dream that died,
A poignant image once hidden inside.

Nectar of the Gods

in loving memory of my father

Amid the bitter sea of reproachful tears,
My spirit sings with a secret joy;
I feel the ecstasy of death blazing through the dark,
Scattering clouds of empty despair.
I float as an angel by the Golden Gate,
Eager to grasp the ascending soul
That assumes the form of my heart's image,
An embedded illusion more real than life,
Free at last from the tyranny of body and time.

Beloved memories bubbling to the top
Are skimmed off for fragrant ambrosia
That is mine alone to sip and savor,
Though hardly daring such indulgence:
Filled with your gentle sweetness,
I smile at your mirrored mirth
And storied offerings drawn from the source's well.

Propelling muse of noble dreams,
Pilot of inspiration,
Raise me up to soar with you on exalted wings.

This is the Way that Love Dies

Watching the sun set between skyscrapers,
Like a coin in the slot of a Wild West show,
I remembered a time
When, tingling like an electric jellyfish,
I stood on the verge of revelation,
Only to find, after racing through
Dusty corridors of labyrinths
In pursuit of vanishing rainbow lights,
That my mind had drifted apart
Like cucumber slices rimmed with ice.

Suddenly to see an impossible moon
Pinned to a deep velvet sky,
Shining with shimmering indigo,
Leering at the love-sick maiden that was.
When the lute strings snap,
Gone is the romance of unrequited love,
Dancing along cords that pull the heart,
Singing an unbearably sweet melody.

This is the way that love dies:
Like a snuffed-out butt in a cut-glass dish,
With stale-wine breath wreathed in body sweat,
And the sickening perfume of wilted lilacs.
The song of the nightingale is of a mocking bird,
And the roses only plastic.

To weep without tears
And scream without sound,
As some internal rupture drains the heart.
To find that no seed has taken root,
Under frothy tower of white bubbles,
Scattered and broken by cold winds,
Leaving no trace of green
Beneath the blank face of water.

The clown who inspired such mirth at parties
Was hung in the closet at home.
While back in little boxes of domestic time,
Two suits of armor, empty beneath the visors,
Sit at opposite sides of a table,
Engage in airy chatter and mechanical duties.
The transparent true self
Still stands shivering and unknown,
Like the sad, silent siren
Who traded her voice for feet.

The nautilus has left her shell
To float unfettered in a vibrant sea,
Bathing in dreams of aquamarine.
But caught by chance, soft and naked,
Sneaking back through the dark hall,
To be scourged by whips of confronting words,
And realize in strange confusion,
That cold emptiness has replaced
A warm home of comforting imagination.

Captured and subdued,
Crushed by rolls of fat,
Split by painful penetration
Invading innermost chambers:
As the mind is de-coupled and sails away,
To know in triumph
That the nightmare demon who reached for the soul
Has only taken the body,
Left behind to writhe like a worm
In the fires of passion.

Forgotten Angel

Cry for the lost child,
The nameless one,
Possibility that never became.
In vain might I search forever
Among all the cherubs of Heaven,
For I would not know the face
Of the little one that was mine.

Fingers of faceless accusers
Point to the murderer,
Standing naked and alone
In an empty hallway of closed doors,
Echoing with whispers of shame.

Cry, cry for the broken heart
Longing for the lost treasure
Thrown so carelessly into a forgotten sea.
Deepest wound that will not heal,
Blood that never ceases to flow,
Tears that will not come
To soothe the burning cheeks;
Sobs buried deep in folds of time
Still ooze and bubble acid regrets.

In the garden of love,

Eden of forbidden bliss,

A monstrous vine has taken root,

And now bears bitter fruit of the grapes of wrath,

Bursting out like a rash of pimples

On the sweet face of Peace,

Each with a venomous viper

Ready to split the skin

And leap out to sink its fangs

Into hands that reach for the harvest.

Bridge of Illusion

Water mirage on the Bird Swamp
Lures thousands of thirsty storks
To the parched gravel of a barren plain,
Respite in the long journey denied;
A rainbow arching up to Heaven
Dissolves before the end is found.

For a few moments of radiant splendor
Clouds are illuminated with edges of gold;
The whisper of a promise
Dances through the air,
Trailing a gossamer cloak of forgotten dreams,
Images suddenly remembered and almost clear
Through the swirling mist.

But before reaching fingers can close,
Everything fades to soft, fuzzy gray;
The brief joy of a soul complete
Buried in dull heartaches of sour memories
And vague longing for lives
That will not return,
Spirits lost in haunting emptiness
That brings on the night.

There are no Roses without Thorns

in memory of my mother

Rise up, golden girl, so tarnished and dull,

Shoulders stooped with care,

That you still may burst through thorny thicket

And shine bright as ancient dawn.

Sail with perfume of freesias

Across waves of heartache,

On tattered wings that beat with the heart

On the long, long journey home.

Although no hero's welcome awaits

In an empty house of faces long turned away,

Assume the dusty mantle

Of all that is noble and good.

Diligently, piece by piece,
From the flotsam and jetsam of time,
Assemble the puzzle of a radiant face,
Blooming with a bright blue smile,
Hidden in a bouquet of roses.

From the underground river of torment,
Take for your own tiny Bonzo dog,
Guardian of memories
That keep the spirit whole.

Roll out the troubled thoughts
Between layers of dough,
Smeared with the butter and lard
Of Mother's baking secrets.

In vain to seek the refuge
Of a lap at last;
No one to gather silver tears
Into their own precious box;
No one to answer the feeble bleats
Of a pale and trembling lamb,
Lost among blades of the field.

Suffocating under a cloud of gloom
That turns everything to cold ashes,
The still unopened bud
Fades on the brittle stem,
Drained of life blood by the gash
From thorns of the fallen queen.

Prayer to the Virgin

Virgin Mary, scorn me not,
Though defiled, besmirched with mud,
Still I reach for purity,
The white-hot flame of burning ice
That transfigures the soul in a blaze of light.
Wash with lilies, scrub with stones,
That the body may become pure as the heart.
Could I but drink with innocent beasts
From that blessed stream,
Purified by the horn of the unicorn,
Tamed by a virgin maid.

Your image, plaster-cast a thousand-fold,
Is weathered by rain and dirt,
Forgotten in an empty world
That laughs in derision at the miracle birth
Of spiritual paternity,
Brought forth in joy, so powerful in glory
That the angels did sing and a star descend
To shine as bright as day.

Crumbled to ruins is the castle of love
That kept the lady of alabaster face
Within perfumed gardens and cloister walls,
My only desire closed in a treasure box,
That she might lean from a balcony high above
To hear a troubadour's poignant song
Of noble and unrequited love,
Warding off swords of armored intruders
From the ramparts of chastity.

Helpless maidens left with no pillar of support
Are forced to trade protective cloaks
For a place in the capitalist machine,
Cheated yet again by men who rule;
Like Ursula's ship full of virgins,
Lost at sea, drifting, buffeted by winds,
As they flee from prisons of marriage,
Only to meet with cruel death
At the hands of barbarian pirates.

Those who snicker in triumph,
So confident in the sower's conquest,
Might heed the quirks of Mother Nature,
Lest they be consumed by black widows,
Spinning silently their intricate webs,
Or cast aside as useless drones,
Limp and passion-spent,
While the great, prolific queen
Glories in her progeny,
Fed on royal jelly and honey
By devoted serving maids.
Sirens who lure men to their doom,
Lorelei who sing temptation,
With faces of beauty, voices irresistibly sweet,
Wield the power of Amazon warriors
By leading to death from denial.

Maiden mother, still unknown,

Mary mild and full of grace,

Earth un-tilled that brings forth fruit,

In you is the promise of eternity.

From bitterness and pain shall come redemption from sin,

Though Cherubim with flaming swords

Still guard the tree of life,

And those who foolishly deny their shame

In flaunting nakedness

Will not be restored thereby

To the Garden of Eden.

Though man toils 'til he turns to dust
To sustain life by the sweat of his brow,
There is no salvation from the fruit of the womb,
No knowledge of good and evil
From the apple of the tree, gift of Eve;
For the harvest is crushed beneath his feet
Into lusty wine for temporal pleasures
Of intoxication and gratification
Of bodily desires.

Let Susanna bathe in innocence,
Free from slander of worldly tongues,
Emerge from the mikvah in purified spirit
To create from immaculate conception,
And float serene on angel's wings
With the Queen of Heaven.

Life in Rose

Dust off the rose-colored glasses,
Look once more through a prism of glass
That lights up the world with rainbow edges.
Put on toe shoes and dance away,
Away from violence and turmoil,
From ugliness and bloodshed,
Away from distorted mirrors
Of other people's eyes,
Away from morbid fascination with cruelty,
From that multitude of empty shades
Who wait for their reflections to appear
On the silver screen,
Leading vicarious lives
Of baseball stars and soap opera queens.

Dare to whisper "magic"
And seek truth in tiny dreams:
Seals in the harbor and blimps in the sky,
Huge melon moon on the plain's horizon,
Mazes through tall reeds,
Chocolate mice and licorice pipes
Hidden in Father's pockets,
Rosebud castles and dragon clouds,
Jewel dewdrops in morning cobwebs,
Baroque cherubs in shafts of light,
Sunset stretching like a golden beach
To a land of forgotten dreams.

Follow the gulls winging high
On a silk scarf of sky
To exotic ports across the sea,
Like a breath in a billowing sail,
Fill with sudden elation,
A whirl of images and sounds,
And float upside down like the Firebird
In a landscape of Chagall.

Fuchsia dream of dancers and Watteau,
Lemon blossom dream of wicker chairs and tea,
Sunflower dream of little girls with china dolls,
Each flower dream not a song unto itself,
But a pure drop of essence,
Distilled perfume of Beauty,
Pieces that fit together somehow
To construct the puzzle of life.

Keys to that secret garden
Where the Queen of Spades reverses to Hearts,
Rise like a phoenix through the flames
From the roots of death.
There at the end of a winding path
Through an amphitheater of roses,
Down stone steps lined with snug succulents,
Draw aside a curtain of moss
And seek answers in the depths
Of a crystal pool.

Feel with one wave the Nirvana
Of complete revelation,
Knowing that symbols are the true reality,
And the God of Creation is created by man,
In his own image, for his own time,
And hears no prayers nor orders plans.
From the solitude of art, then rejoin
The brotherhood of humanity,
That souls may meet on a loftier plane
Where understanding fuses past with present.
Despite stones hurled by unthinking masses,
Content to spout dogmas of their neighbors,
Great philosophers will think and artists create,
Weaving across borders of time and space
The intricate tapestry of Civilization.

Then with the next wave,

Fill with emptiness,

Left with the heartache of faded dreams

That sift through the hands like the sands of time,

Shadows in a doorway

That pass and are gone.

Fumble in the darkness once more for a match

To light the candle of hope.

Silent Prisons

Hush, little bird, don't beat your wings
Against the invisible bars,
But sing in your cage of a broken heart,
Though it be heard as idle chirping.
When panic seizes the fluttering heart,
And choking screams rise to the throat,
Let them dissipate into silent whispers
That float unseen and unheard.

Sacrificial lamb given by her father,
Shrouded in ghostly white of death,
Hair tied up and hidden from view,
A veil that covers her face,
There at the altar in sharp relief
Against the stained glass shards
And naked body bleeding on the cross:
Lost in a champagne haze of love lies,
She does not hear the word "obey,"
She does not see doors close around her,
Nor hear the key turn in the lock.

But the ring, last link of the ankle chains
That claimed as chattel the Jewish bride,
As bridle to horse and yoke to ox,
Secures her to her lord and master,
Forcing bondage ever after.
Submitting in silence, ashamed to show
The fear and pain of intrusion,
While bloody sheets are hung to display
The triumph of conquest.

Every day she must weave the web
Of the wife that binds her in duty,
Realizing in desolation and despair
That the elusive bird of freedom,
The promise that love is all you need
To wear flowers in your hair,
Has flown overhead and is gone.

Innocent maids unknowingly yield
To the cruel deceptions of fashion
That perpetuate myths of the weaker sex:
Lily feet bound from childhood
No longer feel the pain,
As they hobble behind,
Body bowed in perpetual servitude;
Faint and dizzy, laced up tight
In corsets that squeeze out breath;
Tottering in high heels that force tiny steps
And short skirts that invite invasion.
How useless to deny the currents
That flow deep in the social conscience;
They bubble up in moments of anger
As scum rises to the top,
Showing through the seams of garments
Worn and tattered with age.

But still the spirit, mischievous imp,
May find a way to squeeze
Through a crack under the door,
To dance in a fairy ring beneath the moon
And fly through a psychedelic sky of dreams,
Rocked in the soft arms of music,
An embrace without expectation,
Soothing with the deep peace of a mother
Nursing her trusting child.

When the moon's halo of night crystals
Shatters into dust of dawn,
Deliverance dies with the sweep of a harp;
She must slip back into her prison cell,
Numbed by silence of submission,
While electric shocks of emotional reactions
Are tied into knots in the brain,
And ice cubes of memories frozen in time
Bob idly on the surface of the mind.

Estranged

Ships that pass in silent night,
Seeing but not acknowledging,
No flashing lights of reassurance,
No flags of communication,
Deliberately blank and recalcitrant,
Waiting for a signal, a reaching hand,
But knowing it will not be given;
They scowl at each other in cold, damp fog
As each goes its separate way.

Each holds a cruel mirror up to the other,
As the same accusations bounce between them;
Each unyielding, not budging a smidge,
Too proud to admit any fault;
Shields of defense that cover the heart,
Silence and frigid ice of rejection,
Are ready to meet with resistance
The sinking that once seemed so easy
Into comforting warmth;
And the gulf that separates grows ever deeper,
Too wide to throw a bridge across,
Too dangerous to dare,
Too far to melt into nothing.

Irritations that repeatedly rub
On the same places over and over,
'Til the skin is worn so thin
That the slightest prick will puncture,
And the wound spew forth a venomous brew
Of poisonous vipers and toads
That bite with hate and anger.

But through the mist a glimpse
Of an almost forgotten dream:
Sparked by the company of others,
The Scarlet Pimpernel emerges,
The Red Shadow of romance
Who inspired hopeless love.
How can such a man be hiding
In the dull fop lounging at home?
Which then is the illusion and which the reality?
Like a moonbeam that slipped through the hands,
Gone is the shimmer and shine
From the grasp that sought to keep it.

Reap the bitter herbs that were sown,
Dip them in salty tears,
For the sweet honey and milk of a promised place
Has soured in cooling winds.
Hide in vapor that confuses the mind,
Succumb to the numbing cloud:
Cease to fight off the demon of sleep,
Who wraps the soul that suffers in pain
In a cloak of forgetfulness.

Walkabout in the Dreamtime

In the outback bush, fire scars,
Tjukurpa ancestors in the stars,
Heart of stone glows fire red,
Wind whips 'round many heads:
Echoing taps of rrrhythm sticks
By the coolibah, bah, bah,
Goanna go and dingo run,
Blood-red sand and blazing sun,
Distant drone of the didgeridoo,
Boomerang for the kangaroo,

Walkabout, out, out in the dream-time, I'm, I'm.
Walkabout, out, out in the dream-time, I'm, I'm.

Wombat woomera, witchery grub,
Numbat, galah, mulga scrub,
Cuscus, cassowary, crocodile walk,
Bilby bandicoot, brolga flock:
Kookaburra calls and wallaby waits
By the billabong, bong, bong,
Echidna knows, platypus plays,
Koalas clutching in a daze,
Bare feet and dirty rags,
Lazy smiles and dilly bags,

Walkabout, out, out in the dream-time, I'm, I'm.
Walkabout, out, out in the dream-time, I'm, I'm.

Indolence in the puffing haze,
Cruel secrets in hidden caves,
Ancient stories in the rocks,
Designs in ochre, meaning lost:
Painted bodies dance the dark
In corroboree, bee, bee,
Pan-pan-palala hunt Kalaya emu,
Rainbow Wanampi slithers down Uluru,
Poison Liru throws a spear,
Sorry cuts on the face appear,

Walkabout, out, out in the dream-time, I'm, I'm,
Walkabout, out, out in the dream-time, I'm, I'm.
Walkabout, out, out in the dream-time, I'm, I'm.

Mother Hood Reflection
for Lindsay

Come back, little dove, to the sheltering nest,

Lest the harsh sun melt the wax

On your fledgling wings,

And you plunge into the depths

Of a restless sea.

Fade not into forlorn shadows

But stay encased in sunlight,

Shimmering with joy in a childhood moment.

Though mixed with pain of anguish,

Love still flows never ceasing

Around her miracle of creation.

For after the nourishing milk has run dry,

The pelican will feed her hungry chicks

With blood from her own breast.

When hurt responds with anger
And anger with hurt,
Hands slap when they mean to caress,
Words bite when they mean to soothe.
Then too late to enfold in ever-forgiving arms,
Hot tears fall in the dark, unseen
On the cheeks of a sleeping cherub.

In that moment to drift inevitably apart
And reach longingly through the mist
To the boat slipping softly away,
Far from the weathered wharf.

Wending through the cruel maze of time,
Might the prodigal, so full of hope,
Return home at last
To find that no one is there.
As small feet echo through an empty house,
All that is left is a message,
That Mother has gone long ago
To search for her lost child.

As she lies in memory's glass coffin,
Silently sleeping forever more,
Childish fists pound in vain on the lid.
For the cries of heartache will not wake the dead,
Nor reopen the deaf ears and blind eyes
To heal the wounds of the past.

Capturing Bubbles

The call of a crow hangs alone
On bony edge of a chilling wind,
Echo of a long-lost memory
Or reveille of a new dawn:
Turning on a narrow precipice,
To stand first at the promised gateway
To a garden of roses,
Then on the brink of an abyss,
Plunging down to eternal nothingness.

The morning sun bleaches all thoughts to white,
Inexorably peeling back
The frayed edges of my life,
Every step stamping the walk with self-pity.
As the flaming plumage of a phoenix
Mysteriously forms from cold, gray ashes,
Dandelions sway their yellow heads
Through cracks in the cement,
And fairy wings suddenly appear
In oil smears of the gutter.
Then in the tension of a bubble,
Beauty is momentarily captured,
And the spirit soars
On upward flight of a bird.

Searching for messages in the clouds
That shift and change
In pale blue of infinity,
As inevitably as vaporous dragons
Leap tirelessly from sprinkler spouts,
A shimmering rainbow suspended
Above their heads,
So hope for love and faith in beauty
Balance in the air,
Spinning out of line in the dizziness
Of suspended animation,
Before darkness closes
With a choking sob.

Catherine Wheel

New York City Memoir

From dizzying height of sparkling glory
Catherine wheels spin out of control,
Falling down between Roman candles
That stand tall and erect,
Competing to shoot higher, higher.
Dazzling beauty of a shower of sparks
Hangs suspended in air,
And slowly fades as it falls
To ashes to ashes and dust to dust.

Broken on the wheel, Catherine wheel,
Why could the body not roll the same way?

As the unfair Ferris wheel revolves,
The next in line mounts a rocking cradle.
Step right up into glitter and tinsel,
The greatest ride of your life! Excitement!
Step right up to the carnival stage,
Take your place in the spotlight!

Over and over the carriage ascends,
For one brief moment hangs a-top the world,
Gently swaying in the breeze.
Then all too soon the car swings down
And throws its occupant out.

Kicked into the ditch, trapped in the gorge,
Where Public Opinion in the vacuum of a yawn
Alternately approves or rejects
With equal indifference:
Like Mercury, beneath a benign face of healing,
Who trades with one hand and steals with the other.
An audience of vultures from an overhanging ledge
Waits to devour its prey,
Picking apart the spirit in anticipation of flesh,
Continuously screeching their criticisms:
"Too fat! Too ugly! Too cold! Too slow!"
The nourishing stream has long since run dry,
Knowing the walls are too steep to climb,
The castle atop the glass mountain
Can never be reached.

Cast aside, chewed up and spat out,
Opportunity forever lost,
To float in the talent cesspool,
Where a multitude of melting minds
Still sputter and flash sparks of brilliance
Amid shards of broken dreams;
But only the ugliest creatures emerge,
Gross distortions of creation gone awry,
Hideous compositions of diseased imagination.

Broken on the wheel, Catherine wheel,
Why could the body not roll the same way?
What cruel mind devises the mechanics of torture?

Rolling, rolling the Fortune Wheel,
Going through mechanical motions,
Hoping each next rotation will hold
The meaning, security, and joy once invested,
But every time coming up empty,
As it rolls slower and slower
To its inevitable end
Along the thin path of reason
That separates the garden of accomplishments
From the barren waste of despair.

A sad, invisible ghost
Gazes with longing through the windows
Of a warm, bright house where she once dwelled,
Although perhaps by mistake:
But all the doors are now shut fast
And no one can hear her cry.

Falling endlessly downwards,
No solid ground in sight,
Slowly enough to see all that passes,
Grabbing on to hold for a short while,
Clinging with bloodied hands
Scraping at the sill of reality,
The wholeness that really never made sense,
While other hands reach out,
Not to help, but to grab anything you have;
And then to let go forever,
Body, mind, and soul to sink
Into the abyss of itself,
And memory itself forgotten.

Broken on the wheel, Catherine wheel,
Why could the body not roll the same way?

The ducks all cower on their nests,
Afraid to leave their little homes,
For the hunters have assembled and stand in a row,
Guns in hand, aimed at the sky,
To shoot down any that try to fly.
King Kong, transplanted from a foreign land,
Is shot down from the highest tower,
Raw animal power
That would not be enslaved for entertainment.

Atlas upon his crumbling base
Groans beneath the growing weight
Of layer upon layer of human waste.
Will not the Titans at last rebel
And bring back to chaos the illusionary order
Imposed by heightened perception?
The pillars of society no longer support
The canopy of civilization.
Like Hamlet's dilemma to impose logic
On a disintegrating world,
From which all good has slowly leaked out
Through some hidden hole.
Do I think because I am, or I am because I think?

With passive pity the waning moon
Gazes upon the woeful world,
Spinning and spinning but never progressing,
Around and around a dying star,
'Til all creation fades into mists of time,
And time itself is swallowed,
Turning ashes to ashes and dust to dust.

Broken on the wheel, Catherine wheel,
Why could the body not roll the same way?

Patchwork

Vermont Memoir

Follow the line,
Only follow the line
Unrolling into darkness,
Yellow ribbon in a narrow pool of light,
Will it lead out of the labyrinth?

Brush past nightmare chimeras,
Glaring eyes in haunted faces,
Filling corridors of memory.
Hear the waves of a captive sea
Lashing against unseen dykes,
Or the muffled roar of the Minotaur
Still in hot pursuit;
But dare not turn to face once more
The grotesque bull-headed man,
With sharp horns and cruel eyes,
Huge hands to crush and subdue,
Drooling jowls ready to consume
Each maiden sacrificed to pleasure.

Love lost, abandoned faith,
Betrayal of heart and soul,
Left on Naxos with Ariadne,
Key to understanding,
Adrift with the black sail of death
In forgotten seas.

Cling to the line
Stretching on and on,
Traveling through nowhere,
Around curves and over hills.
Will it lead out of the labyrinth
To a place of peace
With an endless beach,
Where calm waters meet clear sky?

Float through an endless tunnel,
Wondering idly where it goes.
Familiar things sit on shelves,
And time does not move.
Grasp one or another in passing
To make some coherent whole,
Sew them together, each little square
Stamped with memories.

Cylindrical silos and rust-red barns,
Cows that dot the meadows,
Apple trees by green-gray hills
Reach humble, gnarled hands,
But the dead deer draped on the shoulder of road
Whispers reproach to intruders.

Can a stitch in time repair the tears,
Run a seam from past to present,
Tuck into forgotten folds
The heartaches of intervening years?

Choose a partner for social dancing,
Trip lightly from one to another.
Dos-à-dos and 'round we go,
Step to the beat of the music.
Will a touch make it real?
Will the mirror reflect
Anything more than shadows?

Tiny, sparkling jewels of snow,
Distant powder-dusted peaks,
Backdrop for a movie set,
Where dream selves dance like marionettes.
Black to white, magenta to green,
Step over doorways on ceilings of seals,
Ride a cloud camel to far-away shores
Of sunset gold and orange.

Alternate realities, different times and places,
Patterns of matching scenes,
People pieces that fit together
Form fragments of a counterpane
Where ideas unroll to actions;
But the broken thread of abandoned goals
Fails to hold them whole.

Follow the broken, faded line
That may yet stretch to eternity,
Through the ever deepening darkness.
Will it lead out of the labyrinth?

Magic Mirror

in loving memory of Karin Dewar

The train chugs along on the tracks of time,
Each chosen carriage now empty,
Over mountains, through dark tunnels,
Winds to an end but not a conclusion.
If it passed through a mirror to a backwards world,
Could everything be re-made different?

Ragged cinder maid sweeps the ashes,
Searching for jewels from her past,
Maybe enough to string together
For a necklace to wear to the ball
And dance with the Prince of Delusion.
She waits in front of the mirror in vain
For transformation to feminine beauty
From a touch of Godmother's wand.
Identity once held in a glass slipper
Lost irretrievably on the steps.

The mirror reveals not the fairest queen,
But an ugly hag consumed with envy.
Narcissus, drawn into self-image,
Never looks up from the lake,
To hear the hopeless call of Echo,
Disembodied voice of love.

No one can hide from the mirror of truth,
For a reflection finds its counterpart
In a still pond, in eyes that look back,
In the darkened glass of a door.

As I gaze deeper into swirling mist,
Nightmares of suffering take shape.
Should I turn away, pretend not to see,
Or watch in frozen horror?
Is it a window into her soul or a mirror into mine?

If I shatter the glass, will I obliterate
The sad, pale face that stares back?
Or can I reach through with bloody hands,
To seize the sinking spirit?
If I bear stigmata, can I lighten her load
And both fly free together?
Or will we both drown in a sea of despair,
Entwined and choking each other?
But is it only to wear the crown
Of nobility in society's Heaven?

Feeble Hope flutters amid the evils
Rising from Pandora's box.
Laughter that skips 'round the edge of a well
Falls like a butterfly with dampened wings
Into a pool of tears.
Floating down a stream of rejected love,
Ophelia, shrouded in melancholy,
Her flowers strewn about, their language mute,
Her eyes closed in death.

Cold, unyielding glass between us,
Tell me, magic mirror,
Is there beauty to reflect?
Can a rose be created
Whose perfume passes through
And returns redoubled in radiant reds?
Can fires of the heart
Make it melt at the touch,
Opening a passage to Dreamland,
To wander amid strange fantasies
In a dream of one's own creation?

Though we run and run and never progress,
In the wood where words are forgotten,
I can walk with a fawn in friendship unafraid,
With gentle, trusting embrace.
The man wearing his newspaper has gone,
And words can mean what we wish.
Help the Knight re-mount the horse of Will,
Impossible projects seem brilliant and clear.

When the White Queen comes,

Wind-blown and bewildered,

I will fasten her shawl, tidy her hair,

Let her sleep with her head in my lap,

Accepting as natural a metamorphosis

Into a wooly sheep.

As we float in a boat,

She knits and I row

Across a crab-filled lake.

When the dreamer awakes,

Will that union vanish,

Forgotten with all other memories,

Leaving only a naked figure,

Posing in front of a mirror?

Cassandra

for Adrienne

Cassandra, Cassandra, howling to the wind,
Agony of knowledge none will acknowledge,
Prophet on a soapbox spouting words no one hears,
As we rush back and forth along the streets
Of our limited lives.
Wherein lies validation for the artist of truth?

Barren branches in a slate-gray sky
Just yesterday wore mantles of diamonds,
Snow Queen's silvery courtiers
Sparkling in the morning rays;
Now vanished from naked twigs
Fairy lamps of sculpted ice
Hanging above the eddies
Of a dark emerald stream.
Fleeting reality of things seen-unseen:
A tree falling in the forest unheard
Is the sound of one hand clapping.

"It's here," she cries, "the truth of the soul,
Self-revelation in ripples of a lake,
Zen of perfumed petals, reddish pink,
Multiplied in tiers of a rose garden,
Oak tree filtering golden light,
Seen through a gate in a long-ago dream."
But no one will come to the window to see
The Unicorn in the garden.

We sit in darkness, staring at pictures on a screen,
Ears plugged with headphones,
Afraid to hear our own thoughts
Echoing through hollow halls,
Playing over and over mundane tunes,
Broken records on a turntable of the mind.

How can we give, sacrifice our own blood,
When we are, ourselves, invisible?
Do we exist without mirrors held by other people?
Will they notice if we walk naked in the street?
Is it wrong to wear blue when others wear red,
Fly on a broom while they ride in cars?

Is existence digital, zero or one,
Judged as "yes" or "no"?
Do we see dots of color juxtaposed
To form illusions of reality?
If the barriers melt and all colors run together,
Will a fabric of unity be woven,
Or only a mudflat, a barren plain,
That cracks in the heat of the sun?

We eat steak with relish and never contemplate
A peaceful cow grazing in green meadows;
We think only of sauces when viewing chickens
Hanging by their necks in the butcher's,
And not of a little bird,
Bright eyes, downy feathers,
Pecking eagerly out of its shell
To burst into sunshine and seeds;
We crush beneath our hurrying feet
A beetle crossing the path,
Don't stop or stoop to see shiny blue wings,
Quivering antennae exploring the ground,
A Wogglebug highly intelligent
In its own tiny world.

Too great seems the burden of individual responsibility,
Connecting to every other life.
How much easier to hide behind dogmas
Of religion, opiate of the masses.
We believe in Jesus, who died for our sins,
Whatever those may be, past and future;
We vigorously defend identity,
However abstract the foundations
Of Original Sin and Life Everlasting:
Symbols to justify actions.

Who are we to question the workings of Fate,
Kismet that cannot be altered,
Divine Plan beyond understanding?
If there is no free will and all is pre-ordained,
Then the Devil made us do it,
And we passively accept beatings and abuse,
For the right partner must be the one chosen.

We read without pity about some other place
Where thousands perished in an earthquake,
And still feel redemption from the miracle
Of a little child swept by great waves,
Left unharmed in a pile of rubble.
The fellowship of Us dehumanizes Them,
And although we execute millions,
We devise gas-chamber death, so quick and efficient,
Erase the past for a brighter future.

But the ghosts return, haunting our dreams,
Sunken eyes still seeking answers.
The voice of Cassandra still rings, still sings,
Song of the infinite spirit.
Embrace the mystery without analyzing,
Mirage in a desert of nothingness,
Shimmering just out of reach.

Sadness adheres to all that surrounds us,
As ice absorbs foul odors.
Sinking into swamps of depression and guilt,
Where decay feeds on decay,
The will-'o-the-wisp that might light our way out
Wanders and hovers, then vanishes,
A memory of joy that suddenly flashes
Is lost in the silence of night.

Can we beg release from Furies who pursue,
Dragging bloody trails of our crimes?
Is it too late to listen, too dark to see?
If we reach out, is there anything to touch?
Human beings are tossed, lost in waves
Of conflicting political agendas.
We keep busy answering the many "how's"
Without ever understanding "why."

The curse of knowing but not being heard
Meets the curse of listening in vain,
Seeing through a window someone shouting,
But not hearing a single sound.
And so drift apart, conundrums unanswered,
One life dissolving in the sea:
Footprints in the sand soon covered by the tide,
Trail overgrown with weeds.

Puffed up like a toad with self-righteous causes,
Propelled by bitter winds,
She leads the attack without looking back
To see no one is following.
Suddenly derailed, halting on the brink
Of a yawning gap between thoughts and deeds,
Deflated, shriveled, wandering lost,
Repeating little actions with no meaning.

They come then, the stragglers, bearing debris,
Broken pieces left behind in the quest,
But the shattered shields and links of mail
Won't hold together as armor.
Seeing no monsters, they shrug and leave,
But in solitude the demons return,
Nightmares of one's own creation,
They mock and jeer with tormenting cries,
Circling in ever closer.

Desolate among the ruins of life,
To stare in disbelief at carefree youth,
Laughing, singing, turning work to play,
Dancing on laundry to make it clean,
A fresh tunic to cover pain and suffering.

Had she not rejected love,
Would Apollo's gift shine
In a golden Oracle all could hear?
But Psyche must love Cupid in the darkness of night,
Feeling, never knowing.

We see as through a glass, darkly,
Swirling visions in a crystal ball;
We hear the wordless voice of music,
But prefer miracles to truth.
We believe that prayer can heal the sick,
A spell can blight the crop,
But can't accept that the world is round
And revolves about the sun.

We who have seen the moon turned inside out,
Revealing black, ugly interiors,
No longer gaze at its reflected light
With longing unfulfilled.

Cassandra, clinging to the form of Reason,
Abducted from Athena's temple,
She who knew the enemy hid
Inside a huge wooden horse,
Walked through the doors to meet a brutal death
She foretold but could not prevent.

Dance with Death

Shrouded figure, fear personified,
I have watched you mow the fields,
Cutting down with your scythe first one, then another,
Laying waste to the gardens of love,
Leaving behind burnt stubble of the past
To be watered by bitter salt tears.
Turn to face me, Oh Lord of the Harvest of Life,
For you and I must dance.

You put a gun in my brother's hands
And sent him off to war,
While you, the laughing puppeteer,
Sucked out the souls of soldiers,
And dangled them on strings of death,
Dancing to your command.
We heard of the horrors: children shot in a pit,
Women raped and murdered,
And wondered, looking at our own bloody hands,
How the innocent could be slaughtered.

For who is the enemy that must be killed?
That shadow behind the trees?
The boy on your lawn, searching for an address?
The man who lies beside you in bed?
Have we made targets out of people,
Ranged by patterns of hate,
Pasting on faces of our fears?
And those who crept home, maimed, ashamed,
Still hid inside their armored tanks.
When I poured love on those empty machines,
I heard your jeering laughter,
So certain that death had conquered life.
I knew then we should dance.

You cheated me out of the first little child,
But I bore the others in defiance.
I picked up baby birds, fallen from the nest,
And tried to make them eat.
But when you came to snuff out their tiny lives,
One escaped and flew away.
I spread protective wings when I saw your evil vapors
Filtering through the fog.
And heard your echoed whispers of children I once knew:
Brainstem tumors, poison berries from a tree,
Crushed by rolling cars, fallen from a bridge,
Drowned in underwater caverns of the sea,
Swallowed too many pills, hung from rafters by a rope.
Ring-around-a-rosy, a pocket full o' posy,
Ashes to ashes, we all fall down!
Come, Death; shall we dance?

I have stared at your grisly, skeletal face
Beneath your darkest black hood,
Seen you beckon bony fingers
And hiss, "Choose your way
To follow those who succumbed before.
Put stones in your pockets and wade into a stream,
Stick your head in an oven, inhale fumes from your car."
As I tottered on the edge of reason, gazing down
Into endless night and night-less end,
I grasped at a memory, a torn fragment of joy,
And thought, "No, Death; we can dance."

As long as there are mirrored minds

There is Heaven to reflect.

We are not lost in a void,

An insignificant lump of earth

Spinning through a vast expanse of stars.

For I have seen Eternity and heard the voice of God,

As expressions of creation transcend time,

In paintings that float through millions of eyes,

In songs of words and wordless songs,

In the note of a violin, starting a phrase,

Swelling to a glorious organ hymn.

When the last grain of my hourglass

Has sifted through its neck,

I will not run nor hide.

When you reach out your hands,

I will hold them in mine,

For you and I, we will dance.

Lucy Indigo

for Rin

Lucy in violet, forever inviolate,
Shielded as hand by glove,
Cloistered in ivory Castle of Love,
Hearing songs of a troubadour dove,
Defending chastity against sword fights,
Invasion of errant knights of nights,
Hours of ours and daze of days,
The lark beats his wings in sunlight rays,
Falling in ecstasy, abandoned to fire,
Heart filled with sweetness melts from desire,
On pedestal of dreams high above.

Lucy in white, pure and bright,
Combination of all that might be,
Geisha powder like blossoming tree,
Delicate porcelain mask wears she,
Encased in multi-tiered, wedding-cake gown,
Face hidden by veil, pale roses for crown,
Snow unthawed, impregnable ice,
Glides like a swan through shower of rice,
Cherubs on clouds still sweetly sing,
Before she is chained by a wedding ring,
Wings that will never fly free.

Lucy in red, in pain and dread,
Staunching the flow of blood,
Fire to harden pots of mud,
Rust to paint the barn for stud,
Bricks for birth and baking bread,
Iron springs for wedding bed,
Chili peppers hang by the door,
Slaughtered lamb lies on the floor,
Conquistadors with swords to steal
Spill Aztec blood for cochineal,
As thorns replace rosebud.

Lucy in yellow, submissive and mellow,
Buttercup melting in sun-
Flowers opening petals undone,
Oozing drops of honey run,
Naked flesh of pared pears,
Rounded, juicy fruit of pairs,
Kernels of corn, sheaves of wheat,
In springtime warmth, bitter lemon made sweet,
Jingling coins of gypsy's belt,
Treasure of daisy chain, Rhine Maiden's geld,
Hair like gold that is spun.

Lucy in green, with joy serene,
New life growing within,
The green and sheen of feather and fin,
All nature courtship rites dance in,
Babies of apricot, apple, and plum,
In shamrock clover, bees will hum,
Weeping willow sweeps the grass,
Lily pads in pond like glass,
Let us leave lettuce leaves
For rabbits 'mid the green corn sleeves
Conjured by summer's djinn.

Lucy in blue, melancholy with rue,
Adrift on the sea, alone,
Forget-me-nots are tossed and blown
Across the waste where none were sown,
Waves repeatedly break on the shore,
Fountain to fill a pitcher to pour,
Terns turn and disappear,
In vast expanse of sky, a tear
Of raindrops falling all unseen,
Blue Willow china, washed and clean,
Shells from birds that are flown.

Lucy in brown with a workaday frown,
In roundelay days of routine,
Gone the time when each lass was queen,
Barren the trees that once were green,
Grains to flour, ground beneath,
Coffee and chocolate, a dried-flower wreath,
Toiling for bread, slave to homestead,
Chop up trees to put wood in the shed,
Digging potatoes out of dirt,
Mud and earth to bury hurt,
Sun-burnt hands never clean.

Lucy in gray, all hope washed away,
Lost in a mist of missed chance,
Lived to obey, to follow the dance,
Like leaden fish with flopping pants,
Caught in a net, on gray deck strewn,
Silver sliver of waning moon,
In fog that fuses sky with land,
Brace of doves hangs from hunter's hand,
In depths of sea, receding light,
Fading color before fall of night,
Slanting rays like lance.

Lucy in black, mourning the lack
Of love, lost and gone for good,
Longing shadows, Grim Reaper's hood,
Witch's cat slipped through the wood,
Played like pawn on chessboard of life,
Captive slave of black-white strife,
Toadstool's ink to write at night,
Craven crows will spread a blight,
Raven's croak in cloak of dark,
Bootblack's end in charcoal mark,
As "could" gave way to "should."

Lucy in violet, still inviolate,
Spirit un-fractured and whole,
Life everlasting, immortal soul,
Song of angels, bells that toll,
Beyond the rainbow, above the earth,
Hidden away from pain of birth,
Invisible ultraviolet rays,
Perfume of lilac, lavender sprays,
In Paradise of innocent dream,
Before diffraction splits the beam,
Escape from woman's role.

The Smile

We set out on the Yellow Brick Road,
Dancing towards the Smile
Of happy suns and singing birds,
Twittering cartoon cadenzas,
Flowers nodding in time to the tune,
Tapping feet in silver shoes,
Through emerald fields of neon green,
Poppies bloom red in our spectacles.

Promises of hope, of love and joy,
Everything your heart desires.
"Trust me," said the Smile, "Buy this and wear that:
Eat one of these and drink two of those!"

But the salesman did not smile
When broken things came limping back,
And pills shrank the arms of our babies.
"It's not my fault: you got what you bought!"
And the Smile became a hideous leer.

Where is the Smile when the trees weep their leaves,
And waves wash sandcastles from the beach,
And scallops that were doors become once more
Empty shells on the ocean floor?
For we are but actors who have played our parts,
Taken our smiling bows,
And now slip quietly out the stage door,
Wrapped in our black cloaks,
Like Jane Avril, silent and sad,
Trudging through desolate streets.

Looking back, there is nothing but faceless heads,
Recorded messages on the phone,
No one responsible, no one who knows more
Than the little piece in front of his nose.

And there is the Wizard, revealed for who he is:

A little man turning wheels behind a curtain.

"How are you today?"

booms the echoing voice,

But the Smile is a mask on a stick.

Fifth Commandment

Banish the ghosts who claw at the heart
With tearing, voracious fangs;
Shed sackcloth and tears,
Burn letters and fears,
Crumpled memories stuffed in the flue.

Honor thy parents who did thee beget;
They sacrificed dreams of glory;
For thy sake, they were failures in life;
Carry that cross forever.
By baptismal font, I thee anoint:
Baby born to disappoint;
Doll in a box, poked full of pins,
For pain, penance, pettiness.

In a castle of wrath, the King of Doom
Shriveled to dust in his counting house,
Not knowing his legacy lay in Spring,
Gentle birds who remembered his song.

Wailing banshee in winding sheet
Wandered through dark, dusty halls.
"Oh pity, Lady Lost, forsaken by all!"
With a shard of evil glass in her eye,
Making everything appear ugly.
Though outside the walls, the sun rose and set
Through clouds of orange and gold;
The moon looked down with a sad, pale face,
An indigo sky full of stars.
Three little girls found her roses in bloom:
They danced and sang in her garden.
But hollowed by bitterness, rue and despair,
She heard not their merry laughter,
Nor saw their sweet faces of innocent joy
Smoothing wrinkles of time.
And the green-eyed snake that ate her soul
Slithered through a crack in the ground.

Love that was, that might have been,
Falling petals, wind-blown wisp;
Balance on the pencil-thin line of present
That holds apart past from future;
Cling to that lifeline, guardrail of now,
Stroke that defines what is.
If I draw my self, it is but a point;
All else has faded away,
In multiple stamps of paling ink,
In discolored hues of gray.

I stood by the coffin mourning my death,
Invisible in shroud of black;
But lifting the lid, saw that nothing was there.
Where was the body taken?

Shadow shut in a drawer
Must be sewn to the heels;
Pixie dust to fly through a window.
Escape from the nursery 'ere Mother comes in
To grab her child to smother.

Daedalus flew on to a strange, distant shore,
Believing his son lost at sea.
But Icharus floated, supported by the wings,
Tossed and turned by waves.
Washing up to land at last,
Might he stretch on earth,
Whole of head, heart, and hands,
Healed by resurrection,
Planting trees bearing blossoms and fruit,
Building wings of his own.

Abandon finally the futile endeavor
To climb up the glass mountain;
Its surface did but serve as a mirror
For those who demanded the quest.
The castle on top, erected by elders,
Disappears in a puff of air;
A mythical apex dissolves into sand,
Commandments of chains fall apart.
Break free from self-imposed bondage,
Self-sacrifice others exploit;
For the destiny of life's journey
Is every step along the way.
The crushing weight of burdens passed down
Can be lifted, the bags set aside;
The holy grail is a chalice of body and soul
That only the self can fill.

Electra

for the Tilted Floor, on the theme of "shoot"

Submerged deep interior sea,
She might have slept forever,
Solitude swallowed in dreams of scenes,
Seeming to fill with bubbles,
Suspended without time or space,
Serpents of fantasy reign;
Submarine volcanoes erupt,
Shooting out fiery dykes,
Electric eels, feel of currents,
Hippocampus windows of memory,
Washes of hot hormone release,
Altering perception.

There was an edge, a crest of waves,
A surface her body remembered,
A motion of swimming through water and air,
Of crawling across rocks and dirt;
Grasping with hands, climbing with arms,
Dancing with feet and legs,
Muscle movement defining consciousness,
Membrane between self and other.

Shaped into love that was lost or denied,
A longing that tugged at her heart;
Emerge from the sea to journey back
To shattered remains of the past,
Taking a box to be held close and shut,
For it defined the limits of life.

The moon floated up like a lost balloon,
Through a baby soft blanket of clouds,
And followed her footsteps across the miles,
Wondering where she would wander,
Waning to a crescent cradle of light,
Casting a golden path,
Over glass waters of midnight blue,
Reflect silver darts of a bridge,
Rimmed all around with twinkling jewels,
A shimmering magic tapestry,
Exuberant burst of fireworks
That flung scattered stars to the heavens,
Before it settled on shores of the bay,
To light the darkened earth.

Sudden brilliance of shooting star
Illuminates the way,
Arrow of Artemis arching through sky,
What does it portend?
A wish on a prayer wheel wafted by winds
Up to the gods in Heaven.
Shoot, shooting, where does it fit
In the deep maze of memory?
For in a labyrinth constructed by time,
No one remembers the way in.

Delicate shoots of tender plants
Pushing up through earth,
To be trampled, ripped out, eaten by slugs,
Blackened by icy snows,
Wilting under a parching sun,
Straining against a gale;
Young branches trimmed, bent into shape,
Roots bound, stunting growth,
An old tree in miniature by gardener's hands,
To be kept in a pot on a shelf.

Chutes and ladders, only a game,
Chess pieces moved across a board,
Queen of Hearts facing her rival, Queen of Spades,
Tarts stolen by knaves,
Rewarded by the glittering King of Diamonds,
Punished by the King of Clubs.
But her mother's game, salvaged from her own childhood,
Was fashioned of snakes and ladders:
A ladder to climb to pick the fruit
Of the knowledge of good and evil;
Entwined in the tree, snake of temptation,
Slide down into private hells.

Familiar figure of fluting Pan,
Piping in the dawn,
On crest of a roof overlooking a stage
Where passions of people play out:
Plea of eternal spirit of youth
Returned at last to her home:
But no one remembered the child who vanished
A hundred years ago.

In multiple creases and folds of time,
Lay buried some truth of mind,
Ugly worm inside its silk cocoon
Showing through tattered seams.
Digging through crumbling ruins,
All objects turn to dust,
In a temple that cannot be rebuilt
Over the bones of the dead.

Kept by her father in castle tower,
Barbara, rebellious, beheaded,
Built a third window for the Holy Ghost,
Betrayed by a shepherd turned to stone;
Behind those same bars of silent wake,
Dwelt the Princess Electra.

Shoot: an act of violence,
Violating another body,
Force to cross a boundary,
Union of submission:
For death of innocence, the innocent die,
Evil to be avenged:
Arrogant father, consumed by lightning,
Struck down by a mother's revenge.

Goddess of chase, chaste Diana,
Mourned the death of a gentle hare,
Killed for thoughtless pleasure of sport
While suckling her young.
Iphigenia, promised marriage,
Sacrificed for blood-lust of war,
Men in armor to bring a woman back
To her lord and husband.
Blood that flows from barren womb,
Protecter of virginity,
That death was loss of childhood,
Leaving Electra alone.

Waiting in solitude, nursing a love
For the father who carved her toys,
Who sang and painted, danced and smiled,
For memory of knowledge he shared.
Illicit love to be crushed, cast out,
Denied as childish fancy,
Leaving a hollow that could not fill,
Endless search, forgotten goal.

A mother whose innocence had been killed,
Jealous of her daughter's love,
Turned to a rational man of science
To take her husband's place,
Murdered him when he returned from war
With his captive prophetess of truth.
Electra waited, watching them move
In circles that grew ever smaller,
Hiding in tangled webs of denial,
Living in secret dread,
That some guileless child in the crowd would cry,
"But the emperor has no clothes!"

A brother who came at last to shoot
The mother afraid to love,
Rejecting her children for glory of self,
For wounds she could not heal:
For that deed, forced to wander the earth,
Pursued by horrible Furies,
Ghastly faces of writhing snakes,
Demanding their price in blood,
Leaving Electra alone, unloved,
Unlovable spectator of life.

When the minuet has ended, masks put aside,
To come face-to-face with a mirror,
And realize one has been dancing alone
To someone else's music.
Can love reach beyond itself
In a shooting forth of sperm?
Can a primary urge be twisted around,
Folded back into the psyche?
Love without respect is a ravenous beast,
A blind monster consuming its prey.
Like Electra, one lives alone,
In solitary prisons of the mind.

Night Train

A distant whistle blows deep harmony of brass,
Major seventh, promised joy in the morning.
But dissonance creeps in, a ninth, thirteenth,
Tritones of anxiety;
No resolution to tonic as it slides half-steps down,
Fading into silence of dark.

I ride the night train through crowded stations,
Searching for something familiar,
Up and down stairs, striving to find
The right platform for unknown destinations,
Speeding through condensed events,
As multiple stories play out.

Disembark in cold, gray dawn,
Under a blanket of fog.
To walk in solitude, step by weary step,
Down a road that leads to memory,
Kicking a cart full of bundled projects
To roll a few inches ahead.

Wind chimes repeat some ancient air,
Off-key intervals in random round,
Tolling bells of sunken steeples,
Lost beneath the sea.

The angry buzz of a chainsaw
Cuts through robin's song.
Severs melody improvisation
Of courting white-crown sparrows,
Drowns out plum blossom ragas,
Scattering petals of notes.

Reverie melts in dreary pools,
Inspiration flakes like scales,
Weightless ideas flutter, falter,
Wispy puffs drift over waste.

There was flight in painting, long ago,
Color spectrum matching shapes,
Redwing blackbird calls weave through willows,
Swan: minor seventh to sixth;
Rain sticks to catch currents of wind,
Free the Firebird, caught in a net.

Pan pipes of innocence, Lydian mode,
Phrygian rise with Aurora,
Fluted Dorian, Locrian temples,
Dancing nymphs of nature,
Fly with fairies in fantasy realm,
A future of soaring horizons.

Why do wings atrophy?
How do stars fall?
When did that house of cards tumble to earth?
What is left in ghost town dust
But raisins shriveled by sun?

Bubbles that Mother took away
To watch her baby cry,
Proving fears, engendering need,
Self-inflicted punishment.

When those balloons pop,
Shards of glass rain down,
Lacerate face and body of mind,
Disfiguring self-image,
Twisting limbs in crooked pose,
Aged hag in mirrors of perception;
Turn in to form a shield,
Throw up walls of defense,
Nursing wounds from shattered dreams.

The night train waits, passengers board,
Perhaps to ride forever,
Into darkness of hidden selves,
Through tunnels of the psyche;
Chromatic chords voice, "All aboard!"
Blue landscape of the soul.

Phantom Riches

All Hallows Eve, when the dead are freed,
Flying Dutchman appears on the waves;
What do they seek, these ghosts from the past,
Restless avenging spirits,
In prisons of bones, decaying flesh,
Eyes that no longer see,
Haunting houses where once they dwelt,
Dragging chains of worldly wealth?

Lure of riches draws ghouls from graves;
Phantom armies still battle for spoils,
While dragons of greed guard treasure troves,
Stolen gold lies under the sea.

What web of desire holds them suspended,
To torture with questions that linger?
Memories of hurt, like trails of blood,
Demand sacrifice for redemption.

Jeweled dagger taken by Aztec priest
To rip out hearts of captives,
Murdered by Spaniard for necklace of gold
To melt into royal money,
Killed by pirates, galleons sink,
Treasure chest buried in sand.

Graves are dug beneath piles of possessions,
Tombs are filled with riches,
Terra cotta soldiers stand silently by
As robbers plunder the loot,
And bodies embalmed wander the earth
In search of their stolen treasure.

With a wish for wealth by monkey's paw
Came death to life and love,
Returning to earth as a mangled corpse
To spread a curse of doom.

Foolish Tzar rots in perpetual Hell,
Toiling slave to evil,
While singing eternal 'round fantasy domes,
Spirit of builder he blinded.

Visions by Ghost of Christmas Past,
Bedecked with crown of holly,
Pudding rich in raisins, mincemeat,
Plum sauce and hidden coins:
Sweet love rejected, traded for cash,
Slipped through the counting house door.

Wedding cake of jilted bride,
Covered with cobwebs and mold,
As she sits in dark, her tattered gown,
Angry fire consumes her soul.

Those who chase rainbows for pots of gold,
Led by laughing leprechauns,
End up in halls of the Troll King,
Where souls are exchanged for riches;
Substitute changelings with eyes that are scratched,
Seeing ugliness as beauty;
Love lost, self-creation denied,
Binding all in a dance of torment.

With the crow of dawn, specters fade,
Disappearing into their graves,
Ward off the curse, cold kiss of death,
With sign of the cross.
Can souls be released to peace of Heaven
Through rejection of phantom riches?
An offering of prayer in the temple of Art
Atone for inherited sins?
Breaking the cycle of suffering on Earth?
For the meaning of life is life.

Ode to Sappho

Rose in bloom preserve for all time, Diana,
Ring unbroken, petals un-torn for Sappho,
Rosy fingered moon of the dawn caresses,
Clear flowing fountain.

In a corner of the night
Sits a huddled soul,
Warming her hands
Over glowing coals.

Embers of anger
From burning memories,
Fanned by fetid breath
Of vengeful breeze.

Congealed blood of wounds,
Eyes drained of tears,
Bruises to the ego
Faded over years.

Mirror pool reflect female body shameless,
Changing shape of moon in its phases rounding,
Nymph of nature, naiad of stream, fresh water,
Dryad of fruit tree.

Brown snakes in Guam
Have eaten all the birds,
Rats bringing plague
Killed more than a third.

Famine stalks a land
Parched by the sun,
Yazidi girls enslaved
Where rivers with blood run.

Bracelets bind the wrists
Of village child bride,
Daughters killed in honor
By elders of the tribe.

Dragon force of life through the mountain winding,
Sacred woman knowledge of plants for healing,
Womb for growth and two breasts to nourish infants,
Power of Gaia.

In winter Hades rules
Through passion underground,
While Ceres, bowed in grief,
Barren fields surround.

Persephone in Hell
Is crushed by sword and chain,
Returning full of seed
Brings the spring of vine and grain.

Euridice of love
Is lost by viper's bite,
Maenads of lust
Destroy the art of light.

Moon Daughter

for Saoirse

Born in a wild cry of freedom,
Mother Moon offered up her child,
Slid to earth on a pathway of silver,
As wolves sang with the stars.

Floating close, she peered through the window,
Lighting the ground all around,
In an aura of sacred blessing.
Voices rose to meet her in song.

Night creatures gathered in awe,
At the edge of a ring of trees,
As eyes of birches kept watch,
Wind whispered through pines.

Snow fairies laid down a soft blanket,
Nightcaps on rounded rocks,
Feather flakes like glistening jewels
To adorn crooked fingers of branches.

Icicles dripped from eaves,
Like beards of Old Man Frost,
Lacy sculptures of crystal ice
Carved by spirits of Earth and Air.

Flowing from frozen pond,

Waterfall hummed harmony;

Pure white of snow and moon,

And wolves sang with the stars.

Time Elapse

time ties me, tyranny of time,
tee, I, me, eye, tea, aye me!
bondage of hours, of days and years,
minute minutes tick by, tick tock,
run around the clock, running laps,
in and out of laps, time elapse (eel apse?)
no beginning, no end,
We must run to stay in place
in a race against the clock!

look back! look back!
time has elapsed!
one o'clock, two o'clock, three o'clock, four,
open a door, dormouse sleeps,
stretch time through space,
floating on air, weightless, wait!
elliptical ellipsis, orbit 'round the sun,
rotate on tilted axis,
day and night, day unite,
solstice, equinox, season to sow,
solstice, equinox, season to reap,
winter, spring! summer, fall!

elongate time, breathe in, breathe out,

(breathe)

take time, give time,

take time, give time,

map the body, action control,

minute hand, second hand, face of the clock,

hour hand, our hands, face the clock!

feet, beat, march in time,

March, April, May, June,

heartbeat of life, beating time,

a-one, a-two, a-one, two, three, four,

one, two, three, four, five, six,

syncopated syncopation, ra, ta ta-aah.

look back, look front, boxed into now!
five o'clock, six o'clock, seven o'clock, eight,
ate? eaten? when did I eat?
breakfast, lunch, dinner, again,
over and over, but never over,
eggs over easy, breakfast, lunch, dinner, again,
tea, always tea time,
'round and 'round the table,
"Twinkle, twinkle little bat,"
"He's murdering the time!"
crumbs in the watch works
from a best butter knife!

watch! work!

watch the time! punch the clock!

wasting my time, your time, their time,

our time, hour time,

second time, third time, fourth, go forth!

time out! time in, just in time,

I'm late! I'm early? I'm right on time!

gaining time, losing time, using time well,

"How doth the little busy bee

improve each shining hour,"

good timing, glad tidings, timely tidiness!

female phases, pull of the moon,

crescent waning, waxing full,

rising, rounding, reaching fingers of light,

monthly time flies...

We must seize the moment!

King Canute, stop the tide!

look back to the past!

time has elapsed!

nine o'clock, ten o'clock, eleven o'clock, twelve,

elves, elfin, fairy ring dance,

midnight, midday, suspended in the middle,

no time in mind,

in dreams, it seems,

memory is free.

Sea Salt

for Gus

Selkie, swim in seas of dreams,
Return as my child in the morning.
For love is held in an open hand,
Let no fist snuff out light;
A nest to rest before each flight,
Let no walls block the way.

Plunge into waves where salt stings the eyes;
Companions will float beside you;
Though giants weep oceans of tears,
'Tis but the water of life;
For salty sea falls as sweet rain
To wash a blood-soaked Earth.

If witch's owls turn fairies to stone,
Sing to set them free;
Shatter bottles where feelings are trapped,
Fill empty silence with laughter;
Dive deep into holy wells
Where timeless tales intertwine.

Trust that darkness is full of light,
As the moon shines through mist;
For healing waters flow into the soul,
'Round rafts that navigate rivers;
Rolling waves grind rocks to sand,
Uniting all in spirit.

Atonal Atonement

Beg forgiveness with major seventh leap,
'Round Midnight, no resolve to tonic:
Melancholy blues move in parallel seconds,
Echoing dissonant harmonies.

If you show me the steps,
Could we dance together?
But would I be me
Or a shadow of you?

Things lost that must be found,
Broken that must be mended:
Variations of scenes repeat in dreams,
But the quest is never the same.

Startled fawns that won't return,
A mother's trust betrayed;
While Farmer slept, all the baby chicks
Drowned themselves in the duck pond.

Agony of blunders that can't be undone,
A past that can't be rewritten,
Leaving a longing to stretch groping fingers,
Searching through cobwebs and dust.

Regret, like a restless wanderer,
Who cannot find the way home,
Cries in the dark, unseen, unheard,
Stumbling through moonless night.

Returning soldier marches on and on,
Through fragments of the past,
Reassembled into something unfamiliar,
As he peers through windows and doors.

Ghosts of painful memories
Slip through trees to block the path;
Futile to pass, as they follow behind,
Impossible to grasp or subdue.

If I remember the steps,
Could we dance together?
When the music ends,
Float on an echo?

Steel Dinosaur Apocalypse

We wait on the edge of dead harbor,
Steel Dinosaurs that once lifted crates,
Trojan Horses waiting for bellies to fill
With warriors to fight a last battle.

We look to the West with unseeing eyes,
Bloodless limbs ready to run,
Released by rising, turgid waves
Washing toxic waste.

We wait on the edge of impending doom
In a world of virtual reality,
Where screens no longer exist to divide
Illusion from real, animation from flesh,
Game and gain from pain.

We wait on the edge of destruction,
Until we ourselves self-destruct:
Fog obliterates horizons,
Skies of sleet gray drizzle rain.

Is the buzz overhead a drone dropping bombs?
Will silence explode with screams?
Will lights extinguish one by one,
As a blanket of darkness descends?

Will Earth herself vomit lava,
Belch out sulfurous clouds?
Upheaval to shrug off the scourge
Of human-inflicted scars?

Sister Water has dried,

Brother Tree has burned;

Millions march to dead-ends,

Where dreams dissolve in tear-gas tears,

Cages, torture, and death.

We wait

on the edge

of

nothing

Hippocampus Homecoming

Moon, her face tipped sideways,

squashed in her shining dish,

Reflects a silver pathway

across a darkened Bay,

Where false stars of airplanes parallel

pulsing city lights,

'Til silent ghosts of clouds,

sailing grim and gray,

Draw a curtain of oblivion

Across her mournful eyes.

As one recovering from illness

to greet once more the day,

Unsteady steps to a window

to anxiously look out:

White fog obscures horizons,

blank canvas, hidden views.

What has been forgotten?

memories remote:

Where was there beauty,

on wings of singing birds?

Was water ever teal blue,
the Bridge a salmon pink,
Bathed in candy stripes of golden
orangest sunrise?
Were blossoms but in a picture book?
plum trees' fairy garb,
Gossamer cloaks draped on bushes,
webs of sparkling dewdrop jewels,
Red berries that brought Cedar Waxwings,
wearing Harlequin masks,
To dance in joyous chorus
'mid tiny white bouquets?

Hippocampus nestled in the brain
like a fetus in the womb,
Entrusted to guard treasures
of memories deep and rich;
Little seahorse who has played me false
Cannot recreate the past.

Meeting again a childhood friend,
excitement of sharing moments
Dredged up from the depths of time,
paraded out for view;
But none of the mental photos match
from paths long ago diverged.

Returning at last to family home
where nothing looks the same;
Roses have withered, soil parched,
scattered rocks collected from streams;
Where do they belong, these broken walls,
fragments of Father's work?
Squirrel lies crushed upon the street,
lame deer hobbles down a path,
Blind raccoon waits patiently at the back door
for sustenance of Last Rites,
Seeking shelter for final repose,
Communion for all near death.

What is the longing that tugs at my heart
drawing me ever inward?
Follow a laughing sprite into the night,
through secret tunnels of dreams,
To climb across balconies falling apart
in theaters with no view of the stage,
Acting a role in an unrehearsed play,
wearing costumes too tight to remove,
Swimming in oceans, precarious cliffs,
Grabbing branches to move against wind,
Searching for trains through crowds of people,
in eateries that serve greasy food,
Animals and children changing shape,
neglected lizards multiply;
What is familiar in cluttered rooms,
in faces that fill strange hotels?

Why do you show me these mixed-up scenes
of memories gone awry?
When there in deepest well of hope
from which spring bitter tears,
Is reflected the gift I yearn to repeat
but never again may receive:
To hold a small child in warm embrace,
my own from womb to breast,
To feel peaceful trust in power to nourish
growth of joyful love:
But Life's river, coursing through my veins
Floats my body on a one-way journey.